ARMED FORCES OF THE UNITED STATES

THE UNITED STATES ARMY

BY DONNA MCKINNEY

TORQUE™

BELLWETHER MEDIA • MINNEAPOLIS, MN

Torque brims with excitement perfect for thrill-seekers of all kinds. Discover daring survival skills, explore uncharted worlds, and marvel at mighty engines and extreme sports. In *Torque* books, anything can happen. Are you ready?

This edition first published in 2025 by Bellwether Media, Inc.

Library of Congress Cataloging-in-Publication Data

Names: McKinney, Donna B. (Donna Bowen) author.
Title: The United States Army / by Donna McKinney.
Description: Minneapolis, MN : Bellwether Media, 2025. |
Series: Armed forces of the United States | Includes bibliographical references and index. | Audience: Ages 7-12 | Audience: Grades 4-6 |
Summary: "Engaging images accompany information about the United States Army. The combination of high-interest subject matter and light text is intended for students in grades 3 through 7"–Provided by publisher.
Identifiers: LCCN 2024016011 (print) | LCCN 2024016012 (ebook) | ISBN 9798893040111 (library binding) | ISBN 9781644879436 (ebook)
Subjects: LCSH: United States. Army–Juvenile literature.
Classification: LCC UA25 .M194 2025 (print) | LCC UA25 (ebook) | DDC 355.00973-dc23/eng/20240410
LC record available at https://lccn.loc.gov/2024016011
LC ebook record available at https://lccn.loc.gov/2024016012

Editor: Rebecca Sabelko Designer: Jeffrey Kollock

Printed in the United States of America, North Mankato, MN.

TABLE OF CONTENTS

PEACETIME DRILLS

EAGLE PARTNER TRAINING

United States Army soldiers are in Armenia for Eagle Partner. This is a peacetime training exercise with Armenian soldiers. They carry out many different drills. They train with weapons. They practice wound care.

The soldiers build their skills by working together. The drills help them stay ready. They are prepared for war.

DEFENDING THE GROUND

The Army is the largest and oldest U.S. military branch. People who serve are called soldiers. They conduct ground **missions**. Soldiers use **vehicles**, aircraft, and weapons.

The **Pentagon** is the Army **headquarters**. Soldiers are assigned to **bases** in the U.S. and other countries. They may move to different places for missions.

U.S. MILITARY ACADEMY

Young people who want to be Army officers can apply to the U.S. Military Academy. This school is in New York.

SOLDIERS
ARMY VEHICLES
PENTAGON

Soldiers use **armored tanks** and **combat** vehicles in ground combat. They also use helicopters, airplanes, and **drones**. Soldiers fight with weapons like machine guns, **mortars**, and cannons.

Soldiers have a wide range of jobs during peacetime. They train for battle. They help people who are affected by **natural disasters**. They carry out peacekeeping missions.

TANKS AND GUNS

M1A2 ABRAMS

M1A2 Abrams are the Army's main battle tanks. These armored tanks carry cannons and machine guns. M2 and M3 Bradley Fighting Vehicles are used to **scout**. They carry **missiles** and machine guns.

M1126 STRYKER COMBAT VEHICLE

NUMBER IN USE 4,466

x1,000 x1,000 x1,000 x1,000 x466

WHAT IS IT? AN ARMORED COMBAT VEHICLE THAT MOVES SOLDIERS AND CARRIES WEAPONS

FIRST USED 2003

NIGHT VISION GOGGLES

Soldiers carry many different types of guns. They wear helmets, boots, and body armor vests. Night vision goggles help them see in smoke or fog.

Soldiers also travel in the air. UH-60 Black Hawk helicopters move wounded troops to safety. They also carry weapons. CH-47D Chinook helicopters carry troops and vehicles.

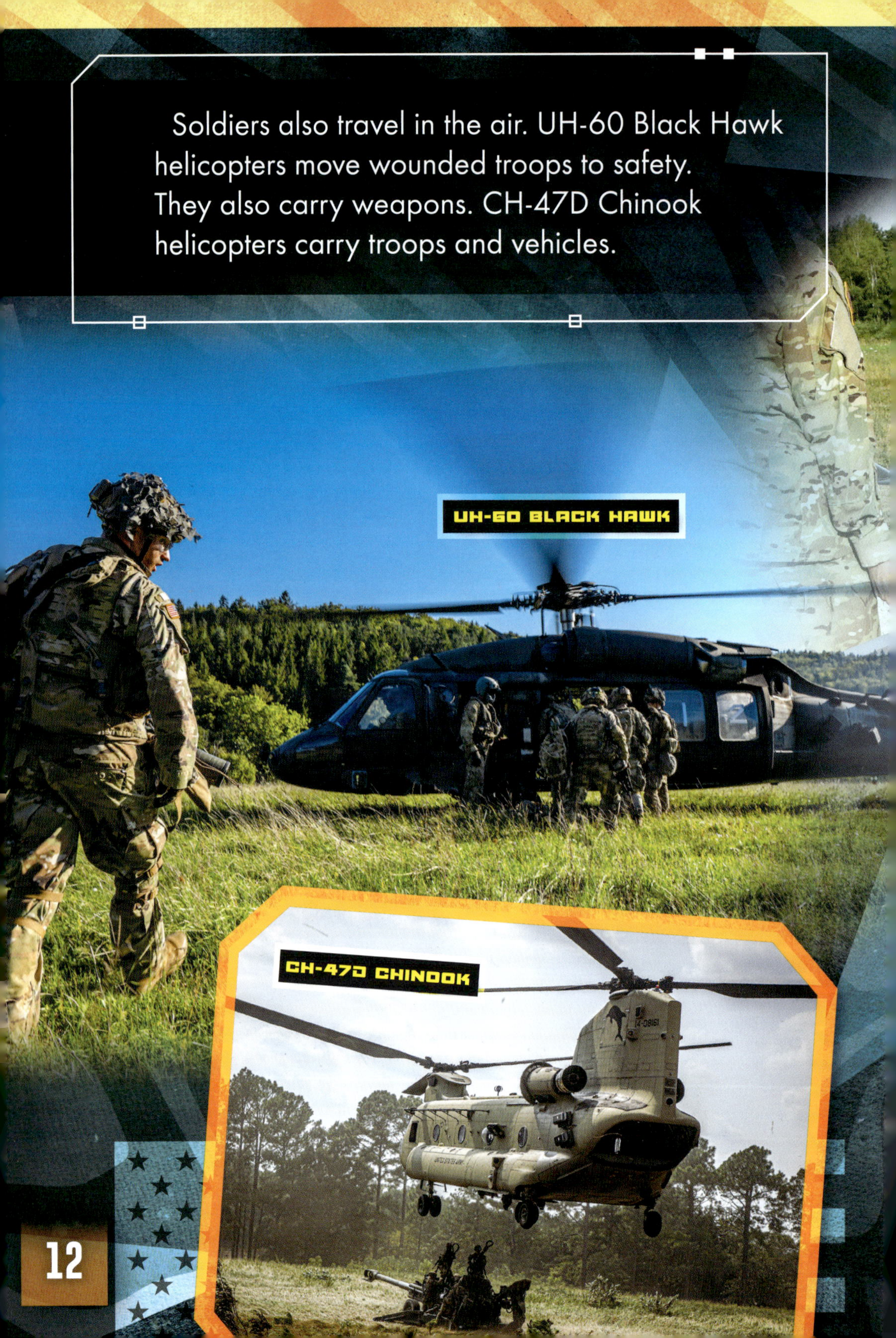

The Army uses drones like RQ-7B Shadows. These aircraft allow soldiers to see battlefields. The Army also uses robotic combat vehicles. These are armed with guns and cannons.

MISSIONS

LONGEST WAR

The Afghanistan War lasted from 2001 to 2021. It is the longest war in American history.

OPERATION ENDURING FREEDOM

The U.S. government wanted to act quickly after the September 11, 2001, **terrorist** attacks. Operation Enduring Freedom began on October 7, 2001. U.S. and British **Special Operations** soldiers went to Afghanistan to help the people fight against the terrorists.

U.S. soldiers entered Iraq in 2003. Their job was to overthrow the **dictator** Saddam Hussein.

MISSION

OPERATION ATLANTIC RESOLVE

DATE STARTED IN 2014

PURPOSE

U.S. ARMY SOLDIERS TRAIN WITH SOLDIERS FROM COUNTRIES IN EUROPE

RESULTS

THE TRAINING KEEPS TROOPS READY FOR COMBAT AND BUILDS PARTNERSHIPS WITH OTHER COUNTRIES

U.S. soldiers have been in Syria since 2015. Around 900 troops are in Syria. They are located in several small bases. Special Operations soldiers also move in and out of the country.

U.S. soldiers help fight terrorist groups. They make it more difficult for terrorists to move supplies. Soldiers also give advice to local troops.

SPECIAL FORCES K-9 UNIT

JOINT TASK FORCE

SOLDIERS TALK TO LOCAL WORKERS WHILE ON PATROL

SOLDIER IN SPACE

Army astronaut Frank C. Rubio flew on the International Space Station for 371 days. He returned to Earth in September 2023. He broke the record for the longest American spaceflight.

A terrible fire burned across the island of Maui in 2023. Soldiers came to assist. They helped search for missing people after the fire. They also delivered supplies to people in need.

The Army is built on a long history of those who have served their country. The Army will continue to be ready to keep the U.S. safe.

ARMY PROFILE

MEMBERS TO REMEMBER

GENERAL DWIGHT D. EISENHOWER
A General of the Army in WWII and later a U.S. president

GRIEST

HAVER

CAPTAIN KRISTEN GRIEST AND FIRST LIEUTENANT SHAYE HAVER
The first women to complete Ranger School

GENERAL NORMAN SCHWARZKOPF
An Army General who led multi-national troops in the Gulf War against Iraq

MISSIONS

WORLD WAR II
1941 to 1945

AFGHANISTAN WAR
2001 to 2021

HURRICANE KATRINA RELIEF
2005

EMBLEM
UNITED STATES
ARMY
LOGO
U.S. ARMY
MOTTO
"This We'll Defend"
YEAR ESTABLISHED
1775
NUMBER OF MEMBERS
active duty in 2022
more than
460,000
RANKS
Private
General

GLOSSARY

armored tanks—large combat vehicles that are protected by thick coverings and that move on tracks

bases—places where armed forces train and work

combat—related to a fight between armed forces

dictator—a person who rules with total power

drones—aircraft that are flown by a remote control or by computers

headquarters—the main office of an organization

missiles—weapons that travel in the air and explode when they hit targets

missions—jobs that Army headquarters assigns to soldiers

mortars—weapons that fire shells

natural disasters—natural events, such as floods, earthquakes, or hurricanes, that cause damage

Pentagon—a building in Arlington, Virginia, that is headquarters for the U.S. military

scout—to look for and track the enemy's position

Special Operations—soldiers trained for the Army's most dangerous missions

terrorist—related to people who use fear to control others

vehicles—machines that are used for carrying and transporting

TO LEARN MORE

AT THE LIBRARY

Leed, Percy. *US Army in Action.* Minneapolis, Minn.: Lerner Publications, 2023.

McKinney, Donna. *Apache Helicopter.* Minneapolis, Minn.: Bellwether Media, 2024.

Noll, Elizabeth. *Armor.* Minneapolis, Minn.: Bellwether Media, 2022.

ON THE WEB

FACTSURFER

Factsurfer.com gives you a safe, fun way to find more information.

1. Go to www.factsurfer.com
2. Enter "The United States Army" into the search box and click 🔍.
3. Select your book cover to see a list of related content.

INDEX

The images in this book are reproduced through the courtesy of: Getmilitaryphotos, front cover, pp. 3, 11; DVIDS, pp. 4, 5 (main, inset), 6, 7 (soldiers, vehicles), 8 (main, inset), 9 (Lewis McChord, Fort Cavazos, Fort Moore), 10, 11 (M1126 Stryker), 12 (main, inset), 13, 14, 15 (left, right), 17 (top, bottom), 18, 19 (top, bottom), 20 (Hurricane Katrina); Jeremy Christensen, p. 7 (Pentagon); Home of the Screaming Eagles/ Wikipedia Commons, p. 9 (Fort Campbell); U.S. Army Corps of Engineers Digital Visual Library/ Wikipedia Commons, p. 9 (Fort Liberty); Lubo Ivanko, p. 11 (goggles); US Army/ Wikipedia Commons, pp. 16, 17 (middle), 18 (fun fact), 20 (Griest, Haver, Schwarzkopf, Afghanistan), 21 (emblem, logo, Private, General); US Coast Guard/ Wikipedia Commons, p. 18 (inset); NA/ Wikipedia Commons, p. 20 (Eisenhower); Pump Park Vintage Photography/ Alamy, p. 20 (WWII); Karlis Dambrans, p. 23.